FRISKY BUSINESS

All About Being Owned by a Cat

Illustrated by: Cathy Jellick

Published in the United States of America
by Hallmark Cards, Inc.

ISBN: 0-87529-636-X

Printed in the United States of America.

CHOOSING THE RIGHT CAT

There are all types of cats.
Decide which would be best for you based
on your lifestyle, needs, and personality.

· CAT TYPES ·

1. Persian   2. Siamese   3. Common Alley   4. Plush, sticks to car windows.

NAMING

Give your cat a name he or she will respond to. Favorite names of cats everywhere include:

1) Your Majesty
2) Your Highness
3) Your Grace
4) Master of All You Survey

5

CAT ACCESSORIES

Owning a new cat requires that you buy the following items:

Water dish, food dish, litter box, cute little bed with "Shhh...Kitty's Sleeping" logo, a couple of ceramic cats, a stuffed cat, a decoupaged cat, a glass cat figurine, several studio-quality cat portraits, a cat bumper sticker or two and cat wallpaper.

COLLAR

A cat collar is a necessary purchase because:

1) It holds an I.D. tag.

2) A leash can be attached.

3) It's soooooooo cute.

CAT QUALITIES

You'll find your cat frisky and fun-loving; you'll find your cat cute and adorable and you'll find your cat in your best linen drawer.

9

THE REWARDS

Owning a cat guarantees that you will always have joy in your heart, companionship in your home and little footprints on the hood of your car.

10

FOOD

It's easy to determine which brand of cat food your cat will prefer. Just go to the store and get the most expensive, hard-to-find gourmet brand. That's the only kind your cat will eat.

WEIGHT

Cats require a carefully planned diet if they are to maintain a sleek appearance and a healthy lifestyle. You know your cat is overweight when:

1) He attempts to rid your house of mice by sending them to Arkansas on vacation land scams.

2) Rather than jumping up onto the seat to drink out of the toilet, he siphons it out with a bendy straw.

3) After polishing off all your rhododendrons, he stares longingly out the window at the elm in the front yard.

DRY CAT FOOD A good, crunchy, dry cat food will add strength to your cat's teeth, luster to his coat, and small, painful indentations to the bottoms of your feet.

WATER

Always keep fresh dishes of water available for your cat. Otherwise, he'll have nothing to slop all over the floor.

FOOD DISH

You, like countless other cat owners, may want to spend the extra dollars to personalize your cat's food dish. However, your cat will still prefer to eat off your plate.

17

DRINKING

You may discover your cat drinking out of the toilet. Don't worry about this. It probably means she has worked up a thirst unrolling and shredding the entire roll of bathroom tissue.

18

CAT TOYS Your cat will have hours of fun batting a ball around the house. Especially if the ball is one of those bell-in-the-middle-and-squeaker-attachments-that-dings-and-squawks-till-you-want-to-kill-kill-kill-the-twisted-maniac-that-invented-it!

COMMENTARY

ching ching ching ching ching ching ching ching ching ching ching ching chi ching chi ching ching ching ching ching ching chi ching ching ching ching ching ching ching ching ching ching ching ching ching ching ching

AMUSEMENT

Your cat will enjoy playing with the following toys:

1) Catnip mouse

2) Ball on a string

3) Your new $1500 Sofa →

LITTER BOX The litter box is a small flat tray that you temporarily fill with litter so that your cat can scatter it all over the room.

UNPLEASANT ODOR

The smart cat owner will keep the litter box someplace inconspicuous where the odor won't be noticeable--like an adjoining state.

SCRATCHING POST

We already talked about the sofa.

COMMUNICATION

To better understand your cat, attempt to learn what certain sounds mean. For example, a gentle purr probably means "I'm hungry," while one short "Meow!" most likely means "I'm hungry." A long wailing sound in the middle of the night usually means "I'm hungry."

GROOMING Your cat will spend hours grooming herself with her tongue. Should you wish to assist, please, use a brush.

FUR BALLS

The fur ball is a small amount of cat hair ingested by your cat in the process of self-grooming. Not to worry. Cats are able to cough up fur balls, and will do so... in the dining room, the next time you're having an intimate dinner.

SHEDDING

During shedding season, try to keep your cat away from dark clothing and fine furniture. Shedding season usually runs from January to mid-December.

BRUSHINGS

Your cat will require a good brushing at least once a week. Though he may enjoy it at first, he will soon indicate that he's had enough. At this point you should finish quickly, otherwise your cat will rip into your hands like a school of piranhas.

...3...2...1...

NEUTERING

As a conscientious cat owner concerned with the pet population explosion, you may wish to have your cat neutered. This tends to be more effective than the "responsibility" lecture.

Before

After

CLAWED OR DECLAWED

To answer this, you should ask yourself how partial you are to drapes, furniture and flesh.

THE VETERINARIAN

Most veterinarians have what are called "Standard Charges." Listed below are a few examples.

Item	Standard Charge
Park in vet's lot	$5
Take pet through vet's door	$25
Vet says "Hello" to you	$15
Vet says "Hello" to cat	$100
Vet says "We'll treat him just like he was our own cat."	$200 and up.

PET CARRIER

There are a few steps you can follow to make using a pet carrier a simple procedure. First, set the pet carrier out so your cat can sniff it and get used to it. Then when you're ready to load your cat into the carrier, have plenty of fresh water and food available. Not for the cat—for you! This attempt could take days!

LIVE CAT

Sniff

FLASH!

PHOTOGRAPHS

It's a good idea to keep a camera and several rolls of film on hand. That way, you'll be able to take hundreds of spontaneous pictures of your cat, all of which look exactly alike.

LEAVING YOUR CAT

When circumstances force you to leave your cat alone at home, you can leave the TV on for companionship. Just be sure to turn the channel to P.B.S., as network programming is way below the I.Q. level of the average cat.

CAT SITTERS When going out of town, one option is to leave your cat with trusted friends. It's best to choose people who are conscientious, mature, and who have no furniture or lamps.

TRAVELLING WITH A CAT

Don't. Trust us on this one.

HIDING YOUR CAT

You may move into an apartment which does not allow pets. If questioned, there are certain phrases that will help hide the fact you own a cat. These phrases include:

1) "That tray full of sand is my tribute to 'Our Friend the Desert.'"

2) "I'm having rodent problems, and that small rubber mouse is a decoy."

3) "I'm a carpet salesman, and what you think is a scratching post is actually a 'sample on a stick.'"

KITTENS

Should your cat have kittens, it's necessary to see that they are given to a good home. The way to define a "good home" is one that will take them.

FREE!

PLANNING FOR THE FUTURE

You may wish to provide for your cat in your will. This is important if your cat has been a loyal companion, if you're concerned about your cat's future and especially, if your relatives are a bunch of lazy, good-for-nothing leeches.

40

BEHAVIOR

Everything About Cat Behavior Explained:

The ancient Egyptians worshiped cats as gods. Cats have never forgotten this.

41

HABITS

On occasion, your cat will stare intently at a particular area on the wall. This usually means:

1) Your cat sees something you haven't noticed.

2) Your cat is practicing meditation techniques.

3) Your cat wants you to get up and look, at which point she'll settle down in the spot you just left.

42

PRECIOUS THINGS YOUR CAT DOES

This would be just about everything.
(And, yes, you will start
involuntarily saying "precious.")

DRAPES Cats commonly claw their way up living room drapes. This behavior has been traced back to primitive ancestral instincts dating back to a time when cats clawed their way up tapestries in castles.

IN OR OUT If your cat is out, she wants in.
If she is in, she wants out.

SLEEP

Your cat will come across a number of places around the house to sleep. These include:

1) The sofa.

2) The carpet by your fireplace.

3) Your face.

EXPLORING

Cats will naturally explore a new environment. For years, it was believed that this was due to innate curiosity. It is now known that they are actually looking for things to destroy while you're at work.

50

NIGHT VISION

Because cats have keen night vision, they can easily walk through a dark house without knocking over a single wastebasket or lamp. The fact that they instead knock over <u>every</u> wastebasket or lamp proves they are doing it out of spite.

CRASH!

meow!

EATING OFF THE TABLE

Eating dinner can be tricky with a cat around the house. At times your cat will probably jump onto the table to nibble at the butter or lick from the gravy boat. To avoid this, keep all dishes covered. This works better than the old "Watch your Cholesterol" speech.

CAT TYPES

To determine whether your cat is an indoor cat or outdoor cat, ask yourself the following question:

"Does my cat prefer to sleep all day in a sunny spot on the bed, or sleep all day in a sunny spot on the lawn?"

a.

b.

A LOST CAT If your cat disappears for several hours or even several days, don't worry. He is probably exercising his natural curiosity by exploring the outdoors, or more likely, he's under the bed, snickering at you in your panicky state.

HOLIDAYS

At Christmastime, your
cat will be fascinated
by the sparkling,
glittering ornaments
on your tree.
He will be fascinated as
he watches them
crash to the ground.

COMMON QUESTIONS

The question "Why do cats chase their tails?" is often asked.

Who knows? Why do they do anything?

WHISKERS

Years of painstaking and extensive research have proven that a cat's whiskers serve no useful or functional purpose -- just like the rest of the cat.

CAT EVOLUTION

Throughout history, cats have evolved and adapted. At the dawn of time they were high-spirited, temperamental, with thick coats of fur. Over the eons, they've developed to become high-spirited and temperamental with slightly thinner fur.

EARLY CAT

This primitive cave drawing depicts the life of the first cat. In 61 million BC, the wheel was invented. Later that same day, the cat curled up and took a nap on it.

HISTORICAL CAT FACTS

George Washington's cat did <u>not</u> have wooden claws.

Lady Godiva's cat did <u>NOT</u> ruin all her clothing.

Marie Antoinette's cat <u>would</u> only <u>eat</u> cake.

Rhett Butler's cat actually said, "I don't give a damn."

MYTHS

The belief that "cats have nine lives" is simply not true. In actuality, cats are just nine times more irritating, annoying, and finicky than any other pet.

63

FEELINGS TOWARD YOUR CAT

How to tell when your love for your cat borders on obsession:

Are you reading this book out loud to him now?

AFFECTION

One way your cat will express affection is by
softly licking the side of your face.
This will most often occur right after she's
eaten a can of liver and sardine cat food.

Each cat has his or her own unique personality. Still, most cat personality types can be broken into three main groups:

1) Aloof, bored and haughty.

2) Bored, haughty and aloof.

3) Haughty, aloof and bored.

COMPANIONSHIP

No, no. You're thinking of a dog.

OTHER PETS Eventually you may wish to buy a "little friend" for your cat. A small dog, perhaps, or another cat. Before you do, ask yourself the following helpful questions:

1) Am I crazy, or what?

2) Am I nuts, or what?

3) Am I out of my mind, or what?

Other books from
SHOEBOX GREETINGS
(A tiny little division of Hallmark)

HEY GUY, ARE YOU: A) Getting Older? B) Getting Better? C) Getting Balder?

WAKE UP AND SMELL THE FORMULA: The A to No Zzzzz's of Having a Baby.

STILL MARRIED AFTER ALL THESE YEARS.

GIRLS JUST WANNA HAVE FACE LIFTS: The Ugly Truth About Getting Older.

DON'T WORRY, BE CRABBY: Maxine's Guide to Life.

EVERYTHING YOU ALWAYS WANTED TO KNOW ABOUT STRESS...but were too nervous, tense, irritable and moody to ask.

40: THE YEAR OF NAPPING DANGEROUSLY.

RAIDERS OF THE LOST BARK: A Collection of Canine Cartoons.

THE MOM DICTIONARY.

THE DAD DICTIONARY.

THE WORLD ACCORDING TO DENISE.

WORKIN' NOON TO FIVE: The Official Workplace Quizbook.

THE OFFICIAL COLLEGE QUIZ BOOK.

WHAT...ME, 30?

YOU EXPECT ME TO SWALLOW THAT?: The Official Hospital Quiz Book.

THE GOOD, THE PLAID, AND THE BOGEY: A Glossary of Golfing Terms.

THE COLLEGE DICTIONARY: A Book You'll Actually Read!

THE FISHING DICTIONARY: Everything You'll Say About the One That Got Away.